# The Grabbing Bird

Rosemary Hayes

Illustrated by Ian Newsham

**CAMBRIDGE**
UNIVERSITY PRESS

Tom and Sophie were in the park with Gran.
Gran sat on a bench and read her book. Tom
and Sophie went off to play.

Suddenly, Sophie stopped and grabbed Tom's arm.
"Look!" she whispered.

Tom looked, then he gasped. "What *is* it?" he said.

On the branch of a big tree sat a very strange bird. It was the size of a chicken, but its feathers were purple. It had a huge yellow beak and big, bulging eyes.

Tom and Sophie crept closer.

"SCREEEEEECH!" The bird had seen Sophie and Tom. It flapped its wings and flew off, but something fell from its beak and landed at Tom's feet.

Tom picked it up. "Oh, it's only a stone," he said. As he was about to throw it away, Sophie stopped him.

"Look!" she said. "It's changing!" The stone became very bright, then it started to glow. When it stopped glowing, the children saw pictures inside it. They saw lots of people bouncing up and down, waving and crying for help.

Tom and Sophie stared into the stone, then
suddenly they started to bounce, too!

"Hey, this is brilliant!" shouted Sophie, as she
bounced to the top of a big tree.

"Fantastic!" said Tom, bumping into a cloud.

"Watch it, Tom!" yelled Sophie. "That bird's coming back."

The strange bird swooped on Tom and tried to grab the stone, but Tom held the stone tightly. "Go away!" he shouted.

On and on they went, bouncing off planets and
moons, and dodging shooting stars. All the time,
the bird flew after them, trying to get the stone.

At last, they slowed down.

"We're landing," panted Tom, pointing to
a big planet below them.

There were lots of people on the planet and they were all bouncing. As Tom and Sophie drifted down, a girl with wavy hair bounced up and hung on to Tom's leg.

"What are you doing here?" she asked in a high, trembly voice.

Tom opened his hand and showed her the stone. "We were brought here by this strange stone," he said.

When the girl saw the stone, she gasped. Then she shouted, "THE STONE! THEY'VE GOT THE STONE FROM THE GRABBING BIRD! WE'RE SAVED!" When they heard that, all the bouncing people cheered.

"We must take it back to the bouncy castle," panted the girl. "There's a special place for the stone there. Once we've put it back, the bouncing will stop."

At that moment, the grabbing bird dived at Tom, but Tom gave a huge bounce and the bird just missed him. "Go *away!*" he shouted.

"Quick," said the girl. "Take the stone to
the castle."

Tom and Sophie were bigger than the planet
people, so their bounces took them further. They
were the first ones to arrive at the bouncy castle.

Three guards met them at the gate. They were all very fat and sleepy.

"We've brought the stone," gasped Sophie, looking anxiously over her shoulder at the grabbing bird.

"Er . . . er . . . follow us," said the guards and, very slowly, they bounced off down a passageway.

At the end of the passageway there was a
tall pole. On top of the pole was a glass case.

"In there," said the guards, pointing.

Tom bounced up to the top of the pole and
opened the glass case. Carefully, he placed the stone
inside the case and closed the door. THUD! Tom
landed on the floor. The bouncing had stopped.

All the other people came rushing into the bouncy castle. "You've saved us!" said the girl with the trembly voice, hugging Tom and Sophie. "You've stopped all the horrible bouncing."

Suddenly, Sophie noticed a flash of purple and yellow outside the window. It was the grabbing bird! She ran over to warn the guards, but they were yawning so much that they took no notice of her. She shook one of them by the shoulders. "It's the grabbing bird again!" she shouted.

But just at that moment, the grabbing bird swooped down and jabbed each of the guards with its beak. They all fell to the floor, holding their bottoms. Then the grabbing bird flew up and stole the stone from out of the glass case.

Immediately, everyone started to bounce again.

"Quick!" said Tom. "We can bounce higher than the others. Let's see if we can catch the grabbing bird." They bounced out of the castle.

"Don't let it get away!" yelled Sophie. She gave a huge bounce and almost caught the bird, but it flapped furiously and she had to let go. It flew on faster than ever.

"I'll get above it," screamed Tom, bouncing high up into the clouds and diving down towards the bird.

The grabbing bird panicked. It wasn't looking where it was going. SMACK! It hit a tree. Its beak stuck in the tree and the stone fell out. Sophie caught the stone as it fell.

When Sophie and Tom arrived back at the castle,
the stone started to glow. Once again, they saw
a picture in it, but this time it was a picture of Gran.
She was searching for them in the park at home.

They both touched the stone. "Take us home,"
they said, then they threw the stone to the girl
with the trembly voice.

As the girl caught it, Tom and Sophie started to spin. They whirled back through space, back past planets and moons, through clouds, until they landed in the park beside Gran.

As they drove home, Tom saw a purple feather flutter past the car window. He opened the window and looked up at the roof-rack. "OH NO!" he said.